I0752814

OUR LITTLE HARRY

Arthur's
JUVENILE
LIBRARY.
Lippincott, Grambo & Co
PHILADA.

# OUR

# LITTLE HARRY,

AND

# OTHER POEMS AND STORIES.

---

BY T. S. ARTHUR.

---

WITH ILLUSTRATIONS FROM ORIGINAL DESIGNS BY CROOME.

PHILADELPHIA:
LIPPINCOTT, GRAMBO & CO.
1853.

Juvenile
Collection

Entered according to Act of Congress, in the year 1852, by
LIPPINCOTT, GRAMBO & CO.
in the Clerk's Office of the District Court of the Eastern District of
Pennsylvania.

STEREOTYPED BY L. [illegible] N & CO.
PHILADELP[illegible]

# CONTENTS.

# OUR LITTLE HARRY.

OUR sweet, wee brother, Harry,
Say, have you seen him yet?
He has a pair of bright blue eyes,
The darling little pet!
And lips as soft and rosy red
As flower-buds in the spring,
And voice as sweet as voice of bird
On upward-bounding wing.

Say, have you seen the dear, sweet boy,
With his wavy, flaxen hair,
And eyes as full of innocence
As eyes of angels are?
He was twelve months old last Monday,
But still he does not walk,
And only says a word or two,
Though hard he tries to talk.

But, I'm sure he'll walk right early, now,
For he stands up by a chair,
And steps out bravely, if Mamma
To take his hand is there;
And I'm sure he'll talk, too, very soon,
For he knows, now, all we say,
And calls Papa, so very plain,
When Papa is away.

He's a very cunning little rogue—
Last evening, while at tea,
Nurse brought him in, and set him down
In a high chair, close by me.
He laugh'd, and crow'd, and clapped his hands,
And tried, just like the rest,
To eat his bread and drink his tea—
And tried his very best,—

But his tea went on the tablecloth,
And his saucer on the floor,
And his spoon glanced past dear Papa's head,
And struck against the door;
While his little hands flew up and down
Like the swift wings of a bird,
And he laugh'd and crow'd in such a way
As you have never heard.

I laugh'd till I could eat no more,
And little Will was wild,
To see the merry mischief shown
By such a tiny child.
Nurse took him out right quickly,
And I guess we'll take good care
How Mr. Harry we invite
Again our meals to share.

But he is not always such a rogue,
He is not always wild,
But looks, and acts, sometimes, as if
He were an angel-child.
Oh! I wish that you could see him,
On the morning of each day,
When Papa reads the Bible,
And then kneels down to pray,—

As Mamma gets upon her knees,
And we kneel round her chair,
Our dear pet-one drops softly down
To join with us in prayer.
He cannot say "Our Father,"
Though very hard he tries,
And lifts, with such a gentle grace,
His heavenly little eyes.

Our darling little Harry!
He's loved the best of all,—
From Mother's calm and thoughtful eyes
I've seen a tear-drop fall,
As, sleeping sweetly on her breast,
The dear, dear child would lie,
And she has look'd long in his face,—
I know the reason why:

I've heard her say to dear Papa—
"This babe's so sweet and pure:
So all unlike an earth-born child,
He will not live, I'm sure."
But Papa always smiles, and says,
"That's just the reason why,
Of all the dear ones given to us,
Our Harry should not die."

Papa is right—sweet Harry!
He's just the one to stay:
His purity and innocence
Will evil keep away.
If James gets cross, or little Will,
And Anna fretful grow—
Bring Harry in the midst, and smiles
On all their faces glow.

# THE COLD-WATER BOY.

---

A BOY named Frank, who had heard a great deal said about the evil of intemperance, was passing the door of a tavern kept by a man who drew a good deal of custom by his agreeable manners and the pleasant way he had of talking to every one. Frank was whistling a lively tune as he went by, and the landlord, who happened to be standing in the door, said to him in a joking, playful way—

"Good morning, my fine fellow! Won't you step in, and get something to drink?"

Now, Frank had some fun in him as well as the landlord, whom we will call Hartley. And he replied in an off-hand kind of a way—

"I don't care if I do."

And he straightened himself up, and walked, with an erect air, as if he were a man, into the bar-room.

"Well, sir! What will you take?" said the landlord, who was always ready to be pleased with any thing a little out of the common order. "A brandy punch, mint julep, sherry cobbler, or a hot whisky punch? All capital drinks!"

There were two or three old tipling customers in the bar-room, idling their time away instead of being at their work. Here was a little novelty for them, and they gathered around the new-comer, pleased as could be at the prospect of something to break in upon the dullness of the hour. If one of them even thought of the dangerous course the lad was apparently entering, it did not occur to his mind, at the same time, that it was his duty to warn him of his folly. All felt like having some sport out of the boy.

"Try a sherry cobbler," said one, speaking up quickly. "Its first-rate."

"No, no," said another. "Nothing like hot whisky punch. Try that."

And one pulled him one way and one another, while the landlord said, with mock gravity—he was enjoying the scene wonderfully—

"Come—come, sirs! Let the gentleman choose for himself. I reckon he knows what's what, as well as any of you. Now sir," addressing Frank, "which will you take?"

Frank had not been in the least confused by all the hubbub his appearance had created; and, as soon as he could get a chance to order what he wanted, said, with the utmost coolness—

"I'll take a glass of Adam's ale, if you please, landlord."

It was a little curious to see how the laugh began gradually to change to the "other side of the mouth," the moment Frank said this.

"Oh! Adam's ale," returned the landlord, doing his best to keep up the little farce he was acting. "Yes—very good drink, that—only a little too weak." And he poured Frank out a glass of pure, sparkling water, which the lad drank off with the air of one who enjoyed it.

"How does it taste?" inquired one of the tipplers, thinking still to throw the laugh off upon Frank.

"Try a little, won't you?" said the boy, with a serious face. "I'm sure you'll like the taste. It makes you feel good all over, and hasn't a particle of headache or fever in it."

"Indeed! So you're a young teetotaller," remarked Hartley.

"I'm a cold water boy," said Frank as he stepped back from the bar. "And, in return for your compliment this morning, invite you to join our army. We'll make you captain."

Frank did not say this pertly, nor impudently, as most boys would have done, but with such a grave good-humour that it was impossible for any one to be offended. The landlord was taken entirely by surprise, and before he could recover himself and renew the attack, Frank bade him a good-morning and retired.

A day or two after, while Frank was passing Hartley's tavern again, the landlord happened to be at the door. He had been a good deal amused by the lad's off-hand manner of treating his playful invitation to drink; and, although sensible that he had obtained rather the worst in his encounter with the cold-water boy, felt very much inclined to have another passage of wit with him.

"Good morning! Good morning!" said Mr. Hartley. "How are you, my little cold-water friend?"

"Right well, I thank you," replied Frank, in his cheerful, good-humoured way.

"Won't you walk in?" said the landlord.

"No, I thank you," replied Frank.

"We've got some first-rate Adam's ale. Won't you have a glass?"

"No, I believe not! I'd rather take it at the pump."

"From the old iron ladle?"

"Yes. That doesn't taste nor smell of brandy."

"As my glass did!"

"Your glass smelt rather strong, landlord," said Frank, shrugging his shoulders and making a wry face; and the taste of the brandy completely spoiled the water."

"Did it, indeed! I'm sorry. But come in—come in! I want to talk with you. You're an odd sort of a little fellow. We'll have a glass washed so clean that you'll neither taste nor smell brandy."

"I don't think you can," replied Frank, smiling as he stepped in. "Hot water will hardly scald out the taste of the vile stuff."

"Vile stuff! Why do you call brandy vile stuff?"

"Because it makes wise people fools, and

strong men as weak as babies. Wasn't it brandy, gin, or some of this vile stuff, as I call it, with another name, that made Mr. Perkins strike his wife and kill her? You know that he is now in prison, and had like to have been hung?"

"He was drunk."

"Water didn't make him drunk. I go to the pump and take ladle after ladle of the clear, cold water; but I never was drunk in my life."

"Nor do people who drink brandy get drunk, unless they take too much."

"But why do they drink it at all?" asked Frank, growing serious.

"Because they are dry."

"Water would answer a better purpose, and they might drink a gallon of it without getting drunk. And then, you know, it is so much cheaper."

"Oh yes. But if everybody drank water only, we landlords would starve."

Frank only shrugged his shoulders.

"Well, my young cold-water man, what do you say to that?"

"Why," replied Frank with a smile, "that it would be much better for a few landlords to starve, or get into some more useful calling, than for a hundred thousand people to die every year from drunkenness. And I am sure, if you will think about it, you will agree with me."

"Who says a hundred thousand people die drunkards every year?"

"Oh! I've always heard that."

"I don't believe it."

"Well. Say fifty thousand; or even twenty thousand. Isn't that number awful to think of."

Although Frank was very ready in all his remarks, yet they were made with the utmost kindness of manner. There was nothing about either his words or the way in which he said them, that could in the least provoke the landlord's temper. And, therefore, the mind of the latter did not become confused by passion. After a pause of a few moments, he said, speaking half to himself—

"Its not as bad as that, surely."

"Oh yes, sir, a great deal worse," spoke up Frank, earnestly; "for death in itself is a small matter compared with the dreadful sufferings in the drunkard's family, and the loss of his soul in the end."

The landlord's face became serious; for the cold-water boy had given his thoughts a new direction. While he stood musing, Frank said—

"Come down to the hall to-night, and you'll hear all about it."

"To the Temperance Hall?"

"Yes, sir."

"Ho! Wouldn't the folks stare!"

"Suppose they did? Would that do any harm?"

"Oh no! I don't care for that."

"Just say you'll come, won't you? Say it for my sake. I know that if you really saw that you were doing evil in the world, you wouldn't sell another drop of brandy. Won't you come?"

"Oh yes, I'll come, if its just to please you. It can do no harm."

And Hartley was as good as his word. The result, however, was rather more than he had expected. He had never read a temperance document, and was therefore ignorant, to a very great extent, of the true facts in regard to the great moral devastation that was sweeping over the land. It so happened, that a lecturer was exhibiting the appalling consequences of intemperance, and he read, from a pamphlet in his hand, statement after statement, from men in all positions, bearing upon the evils of drunkenness. Having done this, he went on to show, in the clearest manner, the responsibility of those engaged in the liquor-traffic. The goodnatured landlord, who had never permitted himself to reflect upon the consequences attendant upon his calling, was forced to think now, and he thought until his knees trembled.

The cold-water boy was there, and his eyes were scarcely a moment at a time off of the landlord. With pleasure did he observe the effect produced. But how gladly did all his pulses bound, when, after the lecturer sat down, Mr. Hartley deliberately arose to his feet, and while the most perfect stillness reigned around him, said, in a slow, distinct, and serious voice—

"I have sold liquor for twenty years; and if all that I have heard to-night be true, I have been the means of doing more evil than the repentance of a thousand lifetimes can atone for. But my eyes are now open; and seeing the dreadful consequences that follow this traffic, I do here solemnly pledge myself to pour all the liquid poison in my bar-room and cellar into the street, at sunrise to-morrow morning."

Mr. Hartley sat down amid shouts of joy.

True to his word, the landlord did as he had said; and you may be certain that Frank, the cold-water boy, was stirring by sunrise to see the first good work of his convert to temperance.

Mr. Hartley now keeps a temperance boarding-house, and he and Frank, as you may suppose, see each other often, and are on the best terms imaginable.

Boys as well as men can do a great deal of good, if they only go the right way about it.

WILLIE AND THE BEGGAR GIRL.

(10) Page 25.

# WILLY AND THE BEGGAR-GIRL.

"AN apple, dear mother?"
Cried Willy, one day,
Coming in, with his cheeks
Glowing bright, from his play.
I want a nice apple,
A large one and red."
"For whom do you wish it?"
His kind mother said.

"You know, a big apple
I gave you at noon;
And now for another,
My boy, it's too soon."
"There's a poor little girl
At the door, mother dear,"
Said Will, while within
His mild eye shone a tear.

"She says, since last evening
She's eaten no bread;
Her feet are all naked,
And bare is her head.
Unlike me, she's no mother
To love her, I'm sure,
Or she'd not look so hungry,
And ragged, and poor.

"Let me give her an apple;
She wants one, I know;
A nice, large, red apple—
Oh! do not say no."
First a kiss to the lips
Of her generous boy,
Mamma gave with a feeling
Of exquisite joy—

For goodness, whene'er
In a child it is seen,
Gives joy to the heart
Of a mother, I ween—
And then led him out, where,
Still stood by the door
A poor little beggar-girl,
Ragged all o'er.

"Please ma'm, I am hungry,"
The little thing said,
"Oh! will you not give me
A small piece of bread?"
"Yes, child, you shall have it;
But who sends you out
From dwelling to dwelling
To wander about?"

A pair of mild eyes
To the lady were raised;
"My mother's been sick
For a great many days:
So sick, she don't know me."
Sobs stifled the rest,
While heaved with young sorrow
That innocent breast.

Just then, from the store-room—
Where wee Willy ran,
As his mother to question
The poor child began—
Came forth the sweet boy,
With a large loaf of bread,
Held tight in his tiny hands
High o'er his head.

"Here's bread and a plenty!
Eat little girl, eat!"
He cried, as he laid
The great loaf at her feet.
The mother smiled gently,
Then quick through the door
Drew the sad little stranger,
So hungry and poor.

With words kindly spoken
She gave her nice food,
And clothed her with garments
All clean, warm, and good.
This done, she was leading
Her out, when she heard
Will coming down-stairs
Like a fluttering bird.

A newly-bought Leghorn,
With green bow and band,
And an old, worn-out beaver,
He held in his hand.
"Here! give her my new hat,"
He cried—"I can wear
My black one all summer:
Its good—you won't care—

"Say! will you, dear mother?"
  First out through the door,
She passed the girl kindly;
  Then quick from the floor
Caught up the dear child—
  Kissed and kissed him again,
While her glad tears fell freely
  O'er his sweet face like rain.

# SPEAK KINDLY.

---

SPEAK kindly to your brother, Henry; kind words are as easily said as harsh ones. See! there are tears in little Charley's eyes. It is but a moment since, that his happy laugh filled the whole room. Are you not sorry, my boy, that a single word, roughly spoken by you, should have chased the sunshine from that sweet little face? I am sure you are. Go and kiss him, and speak to him kindly and gently, and tell him you are sorry for what you said. There—now his tears are all gone, and his dear little arms are around your neck. Never speak harshly to him again, Henry;

nor, indeed, to any one. Kind words are easily said, and they do good to all, while angry words hurt as badly as blows; and, sometimes, a great deal worse.

Words hurt as bad as blows? Oh yes; and, as I have just said, a great deal more. Why, I have seen a little boy, who scarcely ever minded a fall, even though his flesh was sometimes bruised or wounded, weep as if his heart would break at an unkind word. Speak kindly to each other, then, my children.

## GENEROSITY.

"HAS your brother a peach, William?" asked a mother of one of her children, whom she found sitting by himself, eating a large, ripe peach. William looked up, and said—

"No, ma'am, I believe not."

"Where did you get the one you have?"

"Aunt Mary went by the window just now, and handed it to me."

"And you sat down to eat it alone. Was that generous, or selfish? John loves a peach just as well as you do."

"But Aunt Mary gave it to *me*."

"Your aunt was kind and generous to you; but you were not so to your brother

John, or you would have shared your peach with him, and been much happier, in doing so, than in eating it all yourself."

"I will go and give him a part of it, mother. It was selfish in me, and I am sorry for it. John, John! come and get half of this nice peach."

John came running in, and William gave him him half of his peach. Both of the children enjoyed the fruit, and William was much happier than if he had eaten it alone.

# TWO GENEROUS, LOVING CHILDREN.

---

WE met with a story, in reading the other day, which pleased us very much. A father gave his little daughter, Lydia, a large, ripe peach for herself, and a smaller one for her little brother, who was playing in the yard. Lydia went out to give her brother the peach; when she came in, her father said to her—

"Did you give your brother the peach I sent him?"

Lydia blushed, turned away, and did not answer.

"Did you give your brother the peach I sent him?" asked the father again, a little more sharply.

"No, father," said she, "I did not give him that."

"What did you do with it?" he asked.

"I ate it," said Lydia.

"What! Did you not give your brother any?" asked the father.

"Yes, I did, father," she said, "I gave him mine."

"Why did you not give him the one I told you to give?" asked the father rather sternly.

"Because, father," said Lydia, "I thought he would like mine better."

"But you ought not to disobey your father," said he.

"I did not mean to be disobedient, father," said she; and her bosom began to heave and her chin to quiver.

"But you were, my daughter," said he.

"I thought you would not be displeased with me," said Lydia, "if I did give brother the larger peach;" and the tears began to roll down her cheeks.

"But I wanted you to have the larger,"

said the father; "You are older and larger than he is."

"I want to give the best things to brother," said the noble girl.

"Why?" asked the father, scarcely able to contain himself.

"Because," answered the generous sister, "I love him so; I always feel best when he gets the best things."

"You are right, my precious daughter," said the father, as he fondly embraced her in his arms. "You are right, and you may be certain your father can never be displeased with you for wishing to give up the best of every thing to your affectionate little brother. He is a dear boy, and I am glad you love him so. Do you think he loves you as well as you do him?"

"Yes, father," said the little girl, "I think he does; for when I offered him the larger peach he would not take it, and wanted me to keep it; and it was a good while before I could get him to take it."

# KEEPER'S RELATIONS.

AN honest Mastiff, brave and strong,
Was walking quietly along,
When, near a wood, a fox he spied,
A gaunt, gray, hungry wolf beside.
"How glad we are to see you here!"
The fox cried, with a cunning leer.
"The Wolf and I, just as you came,
Friend Keeper, mentioned you by name."
"Me? What of me?" the dog he said,
And raised suspiciously his head.
"We are relations," Fox replied.
"Long years ago, in forests wide,
Beasts dwelt in closest harmony:
Cousins the wolves and dogs; and we
Were cousins too, but not so near.
Our families, as must appear,
If you will but a moment think,
Are kindred by a common link.

The wolf and I a likeness bear,
And you our features plainly wear:
The difference comes from change of place
And habits, in the self-same race.
We to the northward pass'd, where cold
Stinted our growth, as I've been told;
While you forsook the forests wide,
With man in cities to abide.
Now, this being so, why not be friends?
Our mutual interest thither tends."
All this, and more, the wolf declared
Himself to prove was well prepared.

Deceived, the dog invited both
To visit him; they, nothing loth,
At dusk that very evening came:
Ah! Keeper, he was much to blame.
They shared his supper: call'd him kind;
Yet laugh'd aside—he was so blind!
Soon as the darkness gather'd round,
Fox said he must be homeward bound;
Late hours were bad. The dog said, "Stay
A little longer." But away
Both Wolf and Reynard quickly went,
Scarce pausing for a compliment.

Next morning, scarcely had the sun
His journey o'er the heavens begun,
When two half-eaten lambs were found,
With blood and feathers strewn around.
The truth on Keeper quickly flash'd,
And angrily his teeth he gnash'd.
He waited till the day was o'er,
When his relations came once more.
Wolf look'd demure as any saint,
And Fox as free from sinful taint.
Both call'd him "Cousin"—ah! so kind;
But keeper was no longer blind.
"Villains, away!" he growling cried;
And then his jaws he open'd wide;
And two great rows of teeth were seen,
Like sharp and shining spikes between.
Confused, the wretches turn'd away,
They saw 'twas dangerous there to stay;
But keeper follow'd, growling low,
Till past the fold he saw them go;
Till past the hen-roost many a rood,
The lying, thieving villains stood.

# RABBITS.

---

"ISN'T this a rabbit, father?" asked William, holding up an animal that had been brought in from market. "John says it's a hare."

"And John is right, my son; that is the American hare," replied his father.

"But I am sure I heard you call it a rabbit. Everybody calls these animals rabbits."

"True, William. And yet, really, they are hares. The rabbit, though externally and internally very much like a hare, is yet a distinct species, and superior to the hare in point of sagacity. It burrows in the ground, and thus hides itself and its young from its enemies, while the hare forms its residence on the surface of the earth, and remains constantly exposed to its enemies. Hares are found in nearly every part of the earth, but rabbits were originally confined almost entirely to Europe, from whence they have been taken to other countries. Look at a picture of tame rabbits, and then look at the animal you hold in your hand, and you will see that they are different."

"Oh yes, I can see that very plainly. But if our rabbits, as we call them, are only hares, why are they not called by their right name?"

"A first mistake in naming the animal has made the term rabbit so universal that most people believe it to be correct, and it is now almost impossible to change it into the right one."

"I'll call them hares, after this," said William.

"People would hardly know what you meant."

"But they are hares, and ought to be called so."

"When you speak to others, you wish them to understand the meaning of your words," said William's father, "do you not?"

"Oh yes."

"If you say hare, you will not be understood, for the American hare is known as the rabbit. The usages of a country to a great extent determine for us what we should call certain things, or how we should act in certain cases, where no principle of right or wrong is concerned. It is better always to be correct in every thing, but where the usage of a whole country is slightly incorrect, as in this instance, it is better that lads like yourself should abide by it, instead of attempting to introduce a reform, the result of which would be to effect no change of the custom, and lay you open to the unpleasant ridicule of many."

"But you have said that we never should be afraid of ridicule, father."

"Nor should we. And yet, there are few who can bear it without feeling very unpleasant. It is always best not to provoke it lightly, for those who laugh at us are not in a state to receive good impressions from what we may say or do."

"I never thought of that."

"But it is a fact, William; and, therefore, while we should not be afraid of being laughed at, we should not, for a light cause, call down upon us the ridicule of others."

# THE GOOD ARE BEAUTIFUL.

"OH! what an ugly little creature," said a person turning away from a very homely child, with a look of disgust upon her face.

"She will be beautiful in heaven, ma'am," replied a plainly dressed woman, who overheard the remark.

"Will she, indeed!" returned the individual who spoke so lightly of the homely child. "I should like to know how you can tell that."

"In the other life," returned the woman, "the good are all beautiful, and the evil deformed and ugly. No matter how fair a face a person may have had in this life, it will, in the next world, be changed into beauty or ugliness, according as he has been good or evil."

"How do you know this?" inquired the first speaker.

"Any one who opens his eyes may see and know that this will be true," was replied. "Is not the most beautiful face rendered disagreeable when any bad passion is felt and exhibited? And does not the homeliest face become pleasant to look upon when good affections are in the heart? In the other life, we shall all appear as we really are; and, of course, evil passions will deform the face, and good affections make it beautiful. And she will be beautiful in heaven, for she is a good little girl, homely as her face now is."

## THE WORD OF GOD.

"HENRY, what book is that you have in your hands?"

"It is the Bible, mother."

"Oh no, it cannot be, surely."

"Why, yes it is—see!"

"And my little boy to treat so roughly the book containing God's Holy Word!'"

Henry's face grew serious.

"Oh, I forgot," said he, and went and laid the good book carefully away.

"Try and not forget again, my son. If you treat this book so lightly now, you may, when you become a man, as lightly esteem its holy truths; and then you could never live in heaven with the angels. No one goes to heaven who despises the Word of God, which is, in every jot and tittle, holy."

Henry listened with a serious countenance to his mother, and never afterward treated with lightness either the words of the Holy Book, or the Book itself. Let all children who read this, remember what Henry's mother said.

# THE WEATHER PROPHETS.

I.

"IT will rain," said old Gaspar, as upward his eye
He turn'd, and gaz'd long at the threatening sky—
"It will rain, for since morning an east wind has blown,
And swift through the damp air the light scud has flown.
I know by this sign what the weather will be
On to-morrow: so, Edward, take counsel of me,
And let not the reapers put sickle in grain,
For sure as the day comes, 'twill rain—it will rain!"

II.

"I know it will rain," said the sober old wife;
"This sign I have noticed throughout my whole life—
When the leaf of the maple turns white in the breeze,
And the elm and the willow grow pale 'mid the trees,
Few hours pass away ere the clouds, sweeping high,
Pour forth their bright treasures of rain from the sky.
Last night a wide circle was cast round the moon,
Sure sign of wet weather—'twill visit us soon."

III.

Thus spoke the old couple; and Ned, lazy wight,
Believed—for he wish'd to—the prophecy right;
And away to the town for a rare frolic sped,
With thanks for the dark clouds that hung overhead;
While Gaspar still gazed at the thick-mantled sky,
Till he saw the rain falling—though with fancy's eye—

And his dame at the window still linger'd, to see
The leaves turning white on the old maple-tree.

IV.

Sure enough, on the morrow down pour'd the free rain,
While rush'd the east wind through the golden-topp'd grain.
Old Gaspar was right, and his weather-wise wife
Her sign had read truly once more in her life.
"I knew it—I knew it!" said he, looking wise.
"I knew it," said she, turning up her gray eyes.
And "I knew it!" "I knew it!" throughout the dark day,
Old Gaspar and dame, self-complacent, would say.

V.

Thus could they foretell, from the face of the sky,
From the turn of a leaf, from the wind passing by,
If in sunshine the morning would smile on the earth,
Or clouds, bending sadly, weep over its birth.
But the signs of the times they could never discern,
Although in light written wherever we turn.

In the old-fashion'd way they were plodding life's
round,
Believing no better one ever was found.

VI.

In books, Gaspar saw but a cunning device
For wasting both money and time; and the price
Of a newspaper ever had scrupled to pay,
For he call'd it the throwing of so much away.
His taxes he settled with grumbling; but most
At his school-tax he grumbled, for that was all
lost—
He had paid for Ned's figures t' the hard Rule
of Three,
And that had 'most ruin'd the lad, he could see.

VII.

Years and years pass'd along, and old Gaspar
grew older,
And his weather-wise dame felt the winters grow
colder;
While Ned farm'd the land in the old fashion'd
way,
Content with a ton, to the acre, of hay;
Content if the old, worn-out ten-acre field,
Ten bushels of corn to the acre would yield;

And content, when a rainy day came, to ride
down
And have a good time, as of old, in the town.

VIII.

To the last, though life-weary, and feeble, and
bent,
Old Gaspar, the weather-signs noted intent;
But he saw not a sign of dark days drawing nigh,
Though the tokens were many and plain to the
eye:
Farm wasted, stock dwindled, house tottering to
fall,
And Ned a worse wreck, and more wasted than
all—
For rainy days spent in the town, only led
Into drinking, and evils much worse, lazy Ned.

IX.

From the sky, from the tree, from the wind they
could tell,
Whether sunshine or tempest were coming, right
well;
But forgot, amid all—very strange, but yet true—
That on rainy days Ned must have something to
do.

Books, papers, and pamphlets, Ned found not at
home,
So, to kill time, on stormy days, forth he must
roam;
And, as that old fellow, whom Satan we name,
And load at all times with all manner of blame,

X.

For idle ones ever has work ready plann'd,
Ned enter'd his service—a right willing hand.
Such service is paid, but, like apples which grow
By that sea whose dark waves over lost cities flow,
At first the bright wages seemed gold in the clasp,
But turn'd in a moment to dross in his grasp.
And on these poor wages, Ned toil'd, strange to
say!
For the cheating old rascal full many a day.

XI.

At last the old farmer and dame sank to rest—
Not calmly, 'mid sunshine, on Nature's soft
breast;
For storms, unforeseen, swept across their dark
skies,
And tears dimm'd the light of their weary old
eyes.

Mid strangers, in sadness, life's waves ebb'd away—
Mid strangers, unwept, in their death-sleep they lay—
And strangers stood, tearless, above the green sod,
While the preacher committed their spirits to God

XII.

Where was Ned? From the home he had wasted, estrang'd!
In the service of evil most grievously changed!
He wept not, he thought not, he cared not for those
Whose hearts he had smitten with bitterest woes.
For him they had read not the weather-signs well—
Storms came that their wisdom had fail'd to to foretell:
This truth, when too late, e'en by them was descried—
And they mourn'd o'er their error; and, mourning it, died.

## THE PET FAWN.

---

THERE was once a dear child named Ada, who was of so sweet a temper that she only knew how to love: and the consequence was that everybody and every thing that could know her, loved the sweet little girl in return. I do not believe that a servant in her father's family ever spoke unkindly to Ada—she was so good. There are but few of my young readers, I am afraid, that can say so of themselves. Cook scolds, the chambermaid is so cross, and nurse is out of temper, whenever you come near them. Yes, you know all that; but, my young friends, I am afraid it is all your own fault. Now, examine closely your own feelings and conduct, and see if you do not make this trouble for yourselves. Do you always speak kindly to those around you; and do you always try to give them as little trouble as possible?

As for Ada, everybody loved her, and the reason, as I have already stated, was plain; she didn't know any feeling toward others except that of love. Even the dumb animals would come to her side when she appeared. The cat would rub against her, and purr as she sat in her little chair; and, when she went out to play among the flowers, would run after her just as you have seen a favourite dog run after his master. She never passed Lion, the watch-dog, that he didn't wag his great tail, or turn his head to look after her; and if she stopped and spoke to, or put her hand upon him, his old limbs would quiver with delight, and his face would actually laugh like a human face. And why was this? It was because love prompted Ada to kind acts toward every thing. Love beamed from her innocent countenance, and gave a music to her voice that all ears, even those of dumb animals, were glad to hear. Yes, every thing loved Ada, because she was good.

The father of gentle, loving Ada, was a rich English lord—a certain class of wealthy and distinguished men in England, as most young readers know, are called lords—and he had a great estate some miles from London, in which were many animals, among them herds of deer. When Ada was three or four years old, her father went to live on this estate. Around the fine old mansion into which they removed, were stately trees, green lawns, and beautiful gardens; and a short distance away, and concealed from view by a thick grove, was the park where roamed the graceful deer.

Under the shade of those old trees, upon the smooth-shaven lawn, or amid the sweet flowers in the garden, Ada spent many hours every day, one of the happiest of beings alive.

One morning—it was a few weeks after Ada had come to live in this fair and beautiful place—she strayed off a short distance from the house, being lured away by the bright wild-flowers that grew thickly all around, and with which she was filling her apron. At last, when her tiny apron would not hold a blossom more without pushing off some other flower, Ada looked up from the ground, and discovered that she was out of sight of her house, and among trees which stood so thick together, that the sky could scarcely be seen overhead, nor the light beyond, when she endeavoured to look between the leafy branches. But Ady did not feel afraid, for she knew no cause for fear. She loved every thing, and she felt that every thing loved her. There was not any room in her heart for fear.

Still, Ada felt too much alone, and she turned and sought to find her way out of the woods and get back again. While yet among the trees, she heard a noise of feet approaching, and turning, she saw an animal that was unlike any she had seen before. It came up close to her, and neither of them felt afraid. It was a fawn, only a few months old. The fawn looked into Ada's face with its dark, bright eyes, and when she spoke to it, and laid her hand upon its head, the young creature pressed lovingly against the child.

When Ada found her way out of the woods, and came again upon the green lawn, the young deer was close by her side. As soon as Lion saw the fawn, he gave a loud bark, and came dashing toward the timid creature. But Ada put her arm around its neck and said—

"Don't be afraid. Lion won't hurt you. Lion is a good dog."

And Lion seemed to understand the act of Ada, for he stopped short before he reached them, wagged his tail, and looked curiously at the new companion which Ada had found. First he walked round and round, as if the whole matter was not clear to him. He had chased deer in his time, and did not seem to understand why he was not to sink his great teeth into the tender flank of the gentle creature that had followed his young mistress from the woods. But he soon appeared to get light on this difficult subject; for he came up to be patted by Ada, and did not even growl at the fawn, nor show any disposition to hurt it.

The fawn would not stay in the park after this. Ada's father had it taken back once or twice, but before the day was gone, it managed to escape, and came to see its newly found friend. After this it was permitted to remain; and every day little Ada fed it with her own hand. When others of the family approached, the timid creature would start away; but when Ada appeared, it came with confidence to her side.

Ada had a brother two years older than she was. He was different from his sister in not having her innocent mind and loving heart. Sometimes he indulged in a cruel disposition, and often he was ill-tempered. When William saw the fawn he was delighted, and tried to make friends with the gentle animal. But the fawn was afraid of him, and, when he tried to come near, would run away, or come up to Ada. Then, if William put his hand on it to caress it, the fawn would shrink closer to Ada, and tremble. William did not like it because the fawn would not be friends with him, and wondered why it should be afraid of him, and not of Ada. He did not think that it was because Ada was so good, while he let evil tempers in his heart.

"But how could the fawn know this?" ask my young readers. "The fawn could not see what was in William's heart."

No; for if it could have done so, it would have been wiser than a human being. But all good affections, let it be remembered, as well as all evil affections, represent themselves in the face and picture themselves in the eyes; and there is, besides, a sphere of what is good or evil about every one, according to the heart's affection—just as the sphere of a rose is around the flower in its odour, showing its quality. Animals, as well as human beings, can read, by a kind of instinct, the good or evil of any one in his face, and perceive, by a mysterious sense, the sphere of good or evil that surrounds him.

You do not clearly understand this, my young reader; nevertheless, it is so. If you are good, others will know it at a glance, and *feel* it when you come near them. And the same will be the case if your hearts are evil.

Ada's pet fawn stayed with her many months, and nothing harmed it. The horns began to push forth, like little knobs from its head; and afterward it grew up to be a stately deer, and was sent back to the park. Ada often went to see her favourite, which now had a pair of beautiful branching antlers. It always knew her, and would come up to her side and lick her hand when she held it forth.

Such power has love over even a brute animal!

SATURDAY IN WINTER.

(10) Page 62.

## SATURDAY IN WINTER.

OUR tasks are all done, come away! come
away!
For a right merry time—for a Saturday play.
See! the bright sun is shining right bravely on
high;
Make haste, or he'll soon be half over the sky.
Come! first with our sleds down the glassy hill-
side,
And then on our skates o'er the river we glide.

Now Harry! sit firm on your sled—here we go!
Swift—swift as an arrow let fly from the bow!
Hurrah! downward rushing, how gayly we speed,
Like an Arab away on his fleet-going steed.
Hurrah! bravely done! down the icy hillside,
Swift—swift as an arrow, again let us glide.

And now for the river! How smooth and now
bright,
Like a mirror it sleeps in the flashing sunlight.
Be sure, brother Harry, to strap your skates well,
Last time, you remember, how heavy you fell.
Now away! swift away! why Harry! not down?
Are you hurt? You must take better care of your
crown.

Up, up, good brother! now steady! start fair!
Away we go! swift through the keen frosty air.
Down again! Bless me Harry! your skates can't
be right,—
Just wait till I see—no—but now they are tight!
Here we go again! merry as school-boys can be,
From books, pens, and pencils, and black-board
set free.

Tired, at last, of our sport, home to dinner we
run,
And find that two hours ago dinner was done.
But our meat and potatoes we relish quite well,
Though cold, and the reason we scarcely need
tell:
Five hours spent in scudding and skating, I ween,
Would give to such lads as we, appetites keen.

At last the dim twilight succeeds to the day!
Our week's work is ended, and ended our play.
'Tis Saturday night, and we know, with the morn
Another dear Sabbath of rest will be born.
O'er-wearied, we sink into slumber profound,
Assured that God's angels are watching around.

# THE SPECKED APPLE.

MR. ARDEN had two daughters, Jane and Martha, one twelve years old, and the other thirteen, at the time the incident we are about to relate occurred. A little girl named Mary, about the age of Martha, also made one of the family of Mr. Arden. She was the orphan child of a friend, and had been received by Mr. Arden, while quite young, and treated with all the kindness that marked his deportment toward his own children.

Mr. Arden was a man who understood very well that all the unhappiness existing in the world had its origin in selfishness; and that the true way to attain happiness was to seek the good of others. He often explained this to his children, and taught them that in preferring one another in little as well as great things, they would experience more real delight, than in selfishly looking to their own gratification. But this he found a very difficult lesson for young minds to learn. Especially hard did it seem for Jane and Martha to prefer Mary in any thing to themselves. They loved her, because she was a gentle, sweet-tempered girl, and, therefore, they could not help loving her. But they loved themselves better.

One day, late in the winter, at a time when fruit was scarce, Mr. Arden, on coming home from his office, brought with him three large mellow pippins. They were intended for Jane, Martha, and Mary. While at tea, Mr. Arden mentioned the fact that he had three large apples in his coat-pocket for the girls.

"Oh! give me mine," said Jane eagerly.

"Give me mine, papa," said Martha.

But Mary said nothing, although she looked pleased.

"After tea, you shall have them," replied Mr. Arden. "But let me tell you, that there is something about these three apples that will test, to some extent, your characters."

"How can that be, papa?" asked Jane.

"We shall see," replied Mr. Arden, smiling.

"No doubt they will test our love of apples," said Martha, who was a merry little girl.

"Not the least doubt of that in the world," said her father. "But take care, Martha, that, in receiving your apple, you do not lose your appetite for eating it."

"I shall, if it is very sour, or has a poor flavour."

"That you will not find to be the case. They are as fine apples as I have seen for a long time."

"What a mystery papa makes about

these apples" said Jane. "I am really impatient to see them."

"You shall both see and taste them, dear, after tea. But don't forget that there is something about these apples that is going to try your characters."

After they had risen from the tea-table, and the tea things had been cleared away, Mr. Arden brought out his three apples and laid them upon a plate. They were, indeed, tempting to look upon. They were nearly equal in size, but one was less beautiful in shape than the others, and had become "specked," or slightly decayed, on one side of the stem. This defect, though small, was quite apparent.

"They are very beautiful," said the mother, taking the plate in her hand, and examining the fruit. "I think father has neglected me."

"Oh! you shall have half of mine," said Mary quickly.

"And papa shall have half of mine," said Martha.

"And who, then, shall I give half of mine to?" asked Jane. "Oh! I know, I will divide the half of mine between papa and mamma."

"By which means we shall get the largest share," said Mr. Arden. "So, mother, we shall not only fare as well, but better than the rest."

"And that will be all fair, for you ought to have the largest portion always," spoke up Mary, while her eyes expressed the warm affection that was in her heart for her kind benefactors, who had been to her all that her own father and mother could possibly have been.

"Now, Jane," said Mr. Arden, reaching toward her the plate which contained the fruit, "take your apple, dear."

Jane, without pausing a moment, took an apple from the plate.

"Here, Martha," and Mr. Arden presented the plate to his youngest daughter, who took, with a smiling lip and sparkling eye, the large golden apple that her kind father had brought her.

"They have left the specked apple for you, Mary," said Mr. Arden in a slightly disappointed tone. "But, never mind, dear, the ripest and richest fruit is soonest to decay. I have no doubt but that the superior flavour of your apple will more than make up for its slight defect."

The two sisters, who perceived in a moment, from their father's remarks, and the tone in which he spoke, that they had acted selfishly in choosing the best apples for themselves, and that he had noticed it, immediately offered to change with Mary; but she said, with a pleasant smile—

"Oh! no, no. I am perfectly satisfied, I should have taken this one, if I had been offered the first choice."

As she said this, she took a knife from the table, remarking, as she did so, that half of it belonged to Mrs. Arden.

While she yet spoke, she pressed the knife into the apple, but something hard, toward the centre, prevented the blade from going through. A slight pressure broke the apple into halves, and revealed, brightly glistening in the centre, a large and elegant diamond-ring!

"Why, papa!" exclaimed Jane, who understood in an instant what this meant.

"Jane, we are justly punished for our selfishness in taking the best apples and leaving Mary the worst," said Martha, the tears starting to her eyes, even while she made this acknowledgment. "These apples, as father said, have indeed tried our characters. But let me look at your beautiful ring, Mary."

Martha took the ring, and, while examining it, perceived that there was an inscription on the inside. She read it aloud—"*To the least selfish.*"

"It is yours by right, Mary," said Jane, with a generous acknowledgment of what was daily seen by all to be true, "for you are the least selfish here."

Mary said nothing; but her eyes were full of tears.

"My children," said Mr. Arden, "this is a little matter, but it has shown you something of yourselves. I am rejoiced to find that Jane and Martha bear their disappointment in such a generous spirit, for it tells me that the lesson has done them good."

# INVOCATION TO SPRING.

---

I.

NO longer tarry, gentle Spring!
Come, on thy bright and balmy wing!
O'er earth thy rosy fetters fling,
With merry smile!
Come forth!—thy blooming children bring,
And stay awhile!

II.

Come! wake the mock-bird's stirring song,
The lark's rich carol, clear and strong,
The robin's chirp the trees among—
The wren's sweet lay;
Bid all thy choir, a joyful throng!
Here with us stay.

III.

Call out thy lovely offspring round—
Let daisies deck the teeming ground—
The hawthorn hedge-row's bloom be found,
The fragrant rose;
Just smile! and lilacs will abound—
The buds unclose.

IV.

I saw a tender flower look forth,
And smile, from out the fruitful earth,
When fiercely came old blustering North,
With biting blast—
The blossom wither'd in its birth—
Its bloom was past!

V.

Then tarry not, O gentle Spring!
Come, on thy bright and balmy wing!
O'er earth thy rosy fetters fling,
With merry smile!
Come forth!—thy blooming children bring,
And stay awhile.

# INFANTS AND CHILDREN IN HEAVEN.

"FATHER, will sister Jane, who died and went to heaven, always be a little girl? or will she grow up and become a big woman, just as she would have done, if the Lord hadn't taken her away from the earth?"

"She will grow up and become a woman, my dear."

"How can she grow, father? She has left her body here."

"Not her real body, Mary. You know I have told you, that our spiritual bodies are our real bodies."

"And do they grow just as our natural bodies do?"

"Certainly, my daughter. They grow here, and why should they not grow in heaven, where their food is so much better and more nourishing."

"Food! What kind of food, father?"

"Spiritual food."

"What is spiritual food?"

"Any thing thăt satisfies the desires of the mind. The mind must have nourishment, as well as the body, or it cannot grow. Knowledge is the food of the mind. You are always desirous of knowing something. Your mind hungers after knowledge of some kind or other, and is unsatisfied until it gets food. By this it gains strength, and grows gradually, until, by the time the natural body attains its maturity, the mind is also matured. Its knowledge, if of the right kind, becomes wisdom, and the man is a man spiritually, as well as naturally. In heaven, where there are no natural bodies, every thing being spiritual, the real, or spiritual bodies appear before the eyes as our natural bodies appear before our eyes here. And as the little children, who are in heaven, increase in knowledge and wisdom, they must appear to grow, and really do grow, until they reach the full stature of angels."

# CALLING HIS SHEEP BY NAME.

A GENTLEMAN lately travelling in Greece, passed a flock of sheep in his morning walk, and asked the shepherd if it was usual in the Eastern countries to give names to sheep. He replied that it was, and that the sheep obeyed the shepherd when he called them by their names. The gentleman asked the shepherd to call out one of his sheep, and when he did so, it immediately left its pasture and companions and ran up to the shepherd with signs of pleasure, and such ready obedience as he had never before seen in any animal.

Our little readers may have been taught that, in the Bible, natural images are used as the means of conveying spiritual instruction; that, in fact, all natural things are formed from spiritual things, and correspond to them in every particular. They will remember what is said in the tenth chapter of John, about the good Shepherd: "The sheep hear his voice: and he *calleth his own sheep by name,* and leadeth them out. And when he putteth forth his own sheep, he goeth before them, *and the sheep follow him, for they know his voice.* And a stranger will they not follow, but will flee from him: *for they know not the voice of a stranger.*" The Lord says—"I am the good Shepherd, and know my sheep, and am known of mine."

The gentleman of whom we were just speaking, also inquired of the shepherd whether the sheep would come if a stranger called them by name; but he said they would not, but would flee at the voice of a stranger. He said that many of his sheep were still *wild,* for they had not yet learned their names, but that by teaching them, they would all learn them; the others, which knew their names, he called tame sheep.

Remember, dear, little children, that the Lord is your good shepherd, and knows all of your names. You hear his voice and come at his call, when you do good; but you wander from his fold and do not hear his voice, when you do what is wrong. All of you have been taught what it is to do right, and all of you know what it is to do wrong. We hope that none of you are wild sheep, but all know the voice of your good Shepherd, and come when he calls you.

# EVENING PRAYER.

HEAVENLY Father! through the day
Have we wander'd from thy way?
Have our thoughts to error turn'd?
Has within us evil burn'd?

Heavenly Father! oh, remove
Evil thoughts and evil love!
Give us truth our minds to fill;
Give us strength to do thy will.

Often we are led astray
From the true and righteous way;
But, we humbly pray to thee,
From the tempter keep us free.

Heavenly Father! while we sleep,
Angel watchers round us keep:
When the morning breaks, may we
Better, wiser children be.

# A STORY FOR WILLY.

WILLY was a very little boy, only about three years old. But he knew that it was right for him to do what his father and his mother told him to do—and wrong for him to disobey them.

One morning, when mother, brother Thomas, and little sister Margaret had come in to hear father read, Willy began to talk and make a noise.

"Willy, you must sit very still, while I read," said father.

Willy promised that he would sit very still. But as soon as father began to read, Willy began to talk and make a noise with his chair.

Mother tried to make him be still. But Willy was a naughty boy and would not mind. He went on talking and pushing his chair about, and making a great deal of noise all the while father was reading.

Father was very sorry that his little boy was not good, and it made him feel very badly. After he was done reading, he took him up-stairs and locked him up in a room all by himself, and would not let him have any breakfast until all the rest were done.

Then he went up and unlocked the door and let his little boy come out. Willy said he was sorry that he had made a noise, and promised that he would never be naughty any more. And then he kissed his father, and hugged him around the neck tightly, and promised over and over that he would be good next time.

I wonder if he will be good? I wonder if he will sit very still when father reads again in the morning, and if he will kneel down when father and mother kneel down, and be very quiet and good, and, when father says, "Our Father,"—say it over after him very softly.

I hope he will. For his father and mother will love him very much, and what is more, the Good Man will love him very much, and take care of him.

## THE BEAUTY OF GOODNESS.

---

"MOTHER," said a little boy, "I think every good person ought to be beautiful."

"Why so, my son?"

"I cannot explain," said the child hesitating, "but I know what I think."

"You think, perhaps, that the features ought always to correspond to the spirit."

"Yes, mother."

"Well, though you are not old enough to understand all that might be said on this subject, yet there are some things you may be able to see clearly. Have you never known good persons, who have nothing of what is called beauty, yet whose faces are always pleasant to you, because you love them for their goodness?"

"Yes—grandmother's. She is very old, and not very handsome, but she looks always very pleasant to me."

"Do you think you would love her any better, or like to see her more, if she were beautiful?"

"I never think about that—I am always glad enough to see her."

"Well, then, you find that goodness makes the features pleasant—pleasanter, perhaps, than beauty would make them. It is goodness that makes the spirit beautiful, and it is with your spirit you love it. There are some flowers, whose colours and shape are not beautiful, yet their perfume is so delightful that they are general favourites."

"Oh yes," exclaimed the child, "the sweet-scented shrub is one of them."

"And there are some also," continued the mother, "the smell of which is so disagreeable that we avoid them."

"Oh yes, I know several; and some too, that are poisonous."

"Well, then, you see that beauty—mere outward beauty—is of no account; it is, for itself alone, neither to be coveted or loved. The sweet fragrance of the homely shrub you spoke of, corresponds to that influence of goodness which draws our love toward those who have no outward beauty. Such persons will appear in heaven in all the beauty of goodness. And it is there, my dear little boy, that your idea will be realized; there all that is good is of the most perfect beauty."

# TO A CHILD WITH A DOVE.

DEAR child! May dove-like innocence
  Fold its light wings to rest—
As now the bird thou lovest well,
  Upon thy gentle breast,
Fold its light wings, and in thy heart
  Build for itself a nest.

Oh, beautiful is innocence!
  In all its forms we see
A grace that charms, a loveliness,
  A heavenly purity,—
Come, gentle Eden-wanderer!
  Oh, come and dwell with me!

THE DOVE.

Page 92.

## GOD IS EVERYWHERE.

"COME, Edith, and look at the ship sailing out of the bay," said Charles to his sister. "See how gracefully she floats upon the water. She is going far away, thousands of miles, and will not be back for many months."

"Perhaps she will never come back," said Edith, as she came to the window, and stood, with her brother, looking at the noble vessel just sailing out upon the broad, pathless, stormy ocean. "I would not be in her for the world!"

"Why not, Edith?" asked Charles.

"Oh! I am sure I should be drowned," replied the little girl.

"You would be just as safe as you are here," said Charles. "You know, father tells us that we are as safe in one place as in another, for the Lord, who takes care of us, is everywhere."

"But think how many people are drowned at sea, Charles."

"And think how many people are killed on the land," replied Charles. "Don't you remember the anecdote father told us one day about a sailor? There was a great storm and the ship was in much danger. Many of the passengers were terribly frightened, but this sailor was as calm as if the sun were shining above, and the sea undisturbed below. 'Are you not afraid?' said one of the passengers. 'No,' replied the sailor, 'why should I be afraid?' 'We may all be drowned,' said the passenger. 'All of us have once to die,' calmly returned the sailor. The passenger was surprised to see the man's composure. 'Have you followed the sea long?' he asked. 'Ever since I was a boy; and my father followed it before me.' 'Indeed! And where did your father die?' 'He was drowned at sea,' replied the sailor. 'And your grandfather, where did he die?' 'He was also drowned at sea,' said the sailor. 'Father and grandfather drowned at sea!' exclaimed the passenger in astonishment, 'and you not afraid to go to sea?' 'No! God is everywhere,' said the sailor reverently. 'And now,' he added, after pausing a moment, 'may I ask you where your father died?' 'In his bed,' replied the passenger. 'And where did his father die?' 'In his bed,' was again answered. 'Are you not, then, afraid to go to bed,' said the sailor, 'if your father and grandfather both died there?'"

"Oh yes! I remember it very well, now," said Edith. "I know that the Lord takes care of us always, wherever we may be. I know that he is everywhere present."

"And he will take as good care of the people in that ship as he does of those who are on the land," replied Charles. "Father says that we should always go where our duties call us, whether it be upon land or upon sea, for the Lord can and will protect us as much in one place as in another."

# OUR LITTLE SON.

WITHIN our quiet nest at home
  We have a little son;
Five smiling years have pass'd away
  Since his young life begun.
Five smiling years! Brief, happy time!
  So fleet have moved the hours—
So light our steps—we've only seem'd
  To tread among the flowers.

When day declines, and evening shades
  Come stealing soft and slow;
And star-rays in the dusky sky
  But dimly come and go;
From care and thought and business free,
  I homeward turn my feet—
Oh! how the absence is repaid
  When that dear boy I meet.

I do not know that other eyes
  Would linger o'er his face;
Or find on brow, or cheek, or lip
  A single winning grace;
And yet it would be strange, I own,
  If other eyes could see
No beauty in his countenance,
  So beautiful to me.

To us his face is loveliness—
  There sweet expressions blend;
There thoughts look upward; and on these
  Affection's smiles attend.
A picture in our hearts he lives,
  Bound by love's golden frame;
And love has given the precious boy
  A fitly chosen name.

Oh! could we keep our darling one
  As innocent as now;
As free from lines of care and pain
  His smoothly polish'd brow,—
As free from evil every throb
  His joyous pulses fling;
And free each thought that upward soars
  On mind's expanding wing!

O Thou who lovest every one—
  Whose face *their* angels see—
The children Thou hast given to us,
  Hold, hold them near to Thee!
If ever, in their future years,
  Their feet aside should stray,
Oh! lead them gently back again,
  And keep them in Thy way.

# HARRY LEE'S TEMPTATION.

"LOOK here, my lad," said Mr. Gerchem, landlord of the Golden Tankard, speaking to a boy some twelve or thirteen years of age, who was passing his door. The boy stopped.

"A'n't you the son of William Lee, who died last fall?"

"Yes, sir, I am," replied the lad.

"Is this Harry Lee?" said Gerchem in a kind voice, moving a step or two toward the boy, and putting his hand on his head.

"Yes, sir."

"How is your mother, Harry?" inquired the landlord, with much apparent interest.

"She's sick," replied the boy.

"Ah! I'm sorry to hear that. How long has she been sick?"

"Ever since winter. She had to go out a washing, and she took a bad cold. She's been sick ever since."

"Are you very poor?" asked the landlord. The boy did not answer, but looked down at his patched and faded garments. The question needed no oral reply.

"How old are you, Harry?"

"'Most thirteen."

"It's time you was doing something, then, Harry. A boy of your age might earn a dollar or two a week, and that would help your mother very much."

"If I could only get something to do!"

"You can."

"I'm afraid not. I've been going about to the stores and shops for a whole week, trying to get a place. But nobody wants me, unless I'll work for nothing."

"Humph! They are all temperance folks, I suppose. But you needn't look any farther. I want just such a lad as you, and was thinking about you as you came along. I knew your father very well. He was a faithful, industrious man; always true to his employer's interest; and I'm sure his son will be the same. I'll give you a dollar and a half a week; and, after a while, if we agree right well, will make it something better."

The lad's face brightened suddenly, and he said—

"When shall I come?"

"To-morrow morning. Come in for a minute, and I'll tell you what I want you to do."

Harry followed the landlord into his bar-room.

"You see, my son," said Gerchem, in a very kind way, "that I'm all alone here. The young man I had has become a good-for-nothing sot, and to-day I kicked him out of the house to get rid of him. I've determined, as I'm always myself about, to have only a good, smart lad with me in the bar, and I'm sure you're just the one that will please me. You can wash the glasses, and sweep out the bar, and keep every thing in order just as well as any one. And I'll soon teach you to draw a cork or mix a glass of liquor as handily as I can do it myself. And now run home and tell your mother of your good luck. Spruce yourself up in the morning, so as to look as nice as you can, and come round early."

Harry promised to do so, and then left the bar-room, where he had frequently been before with his father, who had died a drunkard. The poor lad remembered, with painful distinctness, the sad degradation of his parent. Nightly would he come home from this very drinking-house, stupid with liquor, after having spent with Gerchem more than half the money received for his day's labour. He had heard his mother say, and well could he comprehend the meaning of her words, that drinking cursed the body and the soul.

Harry felt elated as he stepped quickly from the bar-room of the Golden Tankard, at the prospect of work by which he could earn something to assist his mother, who, though so sick as scarcely to be able to keep about, had to toil early and late in order to get food, raiment, and a home for her little family of three children, of whom Harry was the oldest. But he had only walked a little way when his feet began to linger, and, at last, he stood still and looked very sober. As soon as time had been given him to think, a most unconquerable reluctance to going into a bar-room took possession of his mind. Drinking had brutalized the mind of his father and destroyed his body. He felt that it was a great evil. He also remembered too well the scenes he had witnessed in the room he had just left, when he would go there, late at night, to lead home his drunken parent.

"I don't want to be a tavern-boy," at length fell half-aloud from his lips, as an expression of painful reluctance and disappointment passed over his face.

"But I can get nothing else to do, and I

must work and earn something for my mother," he said, in answer to his own words.

The more the lad thought about and debated this matter in his own mind, the more unhappy did he become. For every reason urged in favour of going, as promised, into Gerchem's bar-room, one as strong in opposition would present itself.

"It is wrong to make drunkards of people," he at last said, in a resolute voice,—"and I cannot go there."

"But mother! I must help her, and I can get nothing else to do," was quickly and sadly responded to this resolution.

Poor lad! He was sorely tried in spirit. He felt that it would be wrong for him to go into a bar-room and sell liquor; and yet, the thin, pale face of his mother was before him, and she seemed reaching toward him her feeble hands and asking him to hold them up.

"Oh! that I could get honest work to do!" said Harry, as he moved on slowly toward his home, almost wringing his hands together as he spoke.

Mrs. Lee, when her son came home, was in bed. Her head was aching so dreadfully that she could not sit up. Harry went and stood by her, and looked into her face until the tears ran down his cheeks, and then he went away to weep by himself. When he had grown calmer, he asked his mother if he should get little Emma and John their suppers of bread and milk. Mrs. Lee said—

"Yes, my son, that's a good boy."

The words were so tenderly spoken that they brought the tears again into the eyes of the kind-hearted, thoughtful lad.

Harry then got Emma and John their suppers; and, as soon as it was dark, undressed them, and laid himself down in the bed beside them until both were fast asleep.

"Now mother," said he, "sha'n't I boil the kettle and make you a cup of tea? I can do it; and it will make you feel so much better."

"There is no tea," returned the mother. "I used the last yesterday." And Mrs. Lee sighed.

Harry sat and thought for some minutes, and then went and hung the kettle on, and kindled a fire beneath it. After doing this, he left the room, went to the house of a neighbour and asked her if she wouldn't give his mother a little tea, as she was sick and the was tea all out. The neighbour was a kind woman, and not only supplied the tea, but stepped in herself and made it for Mrs. Lee; who, after she had drank it, and eaten a little, found herself better.

Harry said nothing to his mother about Gerchem's offer; but he lay awake nearly all night, thinking it over, and trying to search out some reason that would justify his acceptance. Morning found him still undecided, fully, what to do. His mother remained so poorly that she could merely go about, but was not able to work as usual. Harry saw this, and felt more than ever the necessity that required him to do something to earn a little money.

As soon as he had eaten his breakfast, he said to his mother—

"I'm going out again to look for a place. There must be some one who wants a boy that is willing to work."

And away he started. He had promised to go around to Gerchem's early, and he took the direction of the Golden Tankard. On the way he saw a man standing at a shop-door. He hesitated a moment, and then stopping before him said—

"Don't you want a boy, sir?"

"No, I don't," replied the man gruffly.

Harry shrank away, and continued on down the street.

"Oh dear!" he said, pausing suddenly, and speaking in a distressed voice. "I can't go to that place. Indeed, I can't!"

The image of his degraded and besotted father was before the boy's mind. It had arisen every time his thoughts turned toward the bar-room of Gerchem; and seemed to warn him not to enter the place.

"I've promised, and I must go," he remarked to himself, moving on again; "if it's only to tell him that I can't be his shop-boy."

Thus undecided, Harry approached the Golden Tankard. Gerchem had been expecting him for half an hour, and was at the door when he came up.

"You're late, Harry," said the landlord, a little seriously; "but as it is the first time, I suppose it don't matter much. However, I shall want you here earlier. So, come in now, and I'll show you what I want done."

Harry's mind being still undecided, this was a moment of great trial. The liquor-seller turned to go in, but the lad did not follow him.

"Come," said the liquor-seller, turning partly around, and seeing that the boy did not move.

"I—I—I"— stammered the boy.

"What's the matter?" said Gerchem, coming back.

"I—I—I'm afraid—I'm not—I don't know what to do, sir."

"What do you mean?" The landlord frowned.

"I'm afraid it won't be right," said Harry.

"What won't be right? ha!"

"For me to go into your bar-room."

"Indeed! And, pray, why not?"

Harry felt frightened; for the tavern-keeper showed that he was getting angry.

"Liquor makes people drunk; and I'm sure it must be wrong to sell it," said Harry, uttering the first thought that came into his mind.

"You little scoundrel! what do you mean?" exclaimed Gerchem, thrown off of his guard by such unexpected language. Harry started back, as the landlord advanced toward him, and turning, ran away as fast as his feet would carry him. After having gone about half a block, he checked his speed, and walked on slowly, with his eyes upon the pavement, and his heart beating so strongly that he could hear the pulsation in his ears.

"Oh! if I could only get a place," he sighed.

Just then, a man, who had observed the little scene which had passed between him and the tavern-keeper, although he did not comprehend its meaning, came up and said, as he was about passing—

"What's the matter with you and Gerchem, my lad?"

"Nothing," replied Harry, "only he wanted me to go into his bar, and I told him I was afraid it wasn't right to sell liquor."

"Ah!" said the man with surprise at finding such conscientiousness in a lad. "And what made you think it wasn't right?"

"Because it makes people drunk."

"A very good reason. What did he offer to pay you?"

"A dollar and a half a week."

"Do you want a place?"

"Oh yes, sir! Very much. My mother is poor, and so sick she can hardly work at all."

"How old are you?"

"'Most thirteen."

"I think you'll suit me very well," said the man. "I want a good boy; and, if you are willing, will give you a trial. I'm a hatter, and was about advertising for a smart lad to go on errands. If we agree, I will give you the same that the tavern-keeper offered, and raise you to a much better business."

Harry was so affected by this offer, coming, as it did, just as his heart was sinking into despondency, that his voice choked when he attempted to reply.

When he went home, and related the struggle through which he had passed and told of the good situation that had been offered him so unexpectedly, his mother could not help weeping.

"You were right," said she, "my son, to

refuse going to that dreadful place. Nothing but evil could have befallen you there; and all your work would have been evil, and not good to others. If we cannot do good in the world, we must not do harm. You were severely tempted my son; but see the result. At the very moment when, by resisting temptation, you appeared to have suffered loss, your reward came. There is a good Providence over us all, and it will surely be well with us in the end if we turn from evil, no matter how strongly it may allure us."

Harry went to the hatter's, and proved to be an industrious, obedient boy. He has since grown up, and is now a master workman, doing a good business; and the highest pleasure he has, is that which he derives from the fact that he is able to make peaceful the declining years of his mother, for whom he cared so early.

Gerchem died years ago; and of that fearful disease known as the drunkard's madness.

# THE MINER.

DOWN where the daylight never comes
  Toileth the miner on;
He sees not the golden morning break—
  He sees not the setting sun.

Dimly his lamp in the dark vault burns,
  And he sits on the mine's hard floor,
Toiling, toiling, toiling on;
  Toiling for precious ore!

The air is wet; for the dew and rain,
  Drank by the thirsty ground,
Have won their way to his dark retreat,
  And are trickling all around—

And sickly vapours are near his lips;
  And close to his wire-net lamp,
Unseen, as an evil spirit comes,
  Up stealeth the dread fire-damp!

But the miner works on, though death is by,
  And fears not the monster grim;
For the wiry gauze, round his steady light,
  Makes a safety-lamp for him.

Rough and rude, and of little worth,
  Seems the ore that the miner brings
From the hidden places where lie conceal'd
  Earth's rare and precious things;

But, tried awhile in the glowing fire,
  It is rough and rude no more;
Art moulds the iron, and forms the gold,
  And fashions the silver ore,—

And useful, rare, and beautiful things
  'Neath the hand of skill arise:
Oh! a thousand, thousand human wants
  The miner's toil supplies!

## HOW TO BE HAPPY.

"OH, I am so tired! I wish I had something to do!" said Jane Thompson to her mother, one day.

"Then why don't you read?" asked her mother. "You have books."

"I'm tired of reading, and I'm tired of every thing."

"You are a very unhappy girl, Jane," said her mother.

"If I am, I can't help it," replied Jane.

"But I am sure you could help it, if you would try, my daughter."

"How can I help it, mother? I am sure I should like very much to know."

"By trying to be useful to others, my daughter."

"So you have said before. But I can't see any thing so very pleasant in working for others. Nobody thinks of being useful to me."

"That is a very selfish thought, Jane," her mother replied in a serious tone, "and the feeling that prompted that thought is the cause of all your unhappiness. You must cease to think only of yourself, and have some kind of regard for others, or you will never be happy."

Jane did not understand her mother, and therefore could see no force in what she said. And her mother perceived this, and so said no more then upon the subject.

About an hour afterward she came into the room, where Jane sat idle and moping, and said—

"Come, Jane, I want you to walk out with me."

"I don't care much about going, mother," Jane replied. "And, if you are willing, would rather stay at home."

"But I wish you to go with me, Jane;

so come, dress yourself as quickly as you can, for you know it never takes me long to get ready."

Jane reluctantly obeyed, and, when dressed, went out with her mother. She felt listless and unhappy, for her mind was not employed upon any subject of interest.

After walking for some ten or fifteen minutes, her mother stopped at a low frame building, and knocked at the door.

"What are you going in there for?" Jane asked in surprise.

"I want to see a poor, sick woman, who lives here," said her mother, in a quiet tone.

"Oh I wish I had stayed at home!" But before Jane could say any more, the knock was answered by a little girl about ten years old, whose uncombed head, soiled clothes and skin, showed that she needed the care of a mother's willing heart and ready hand.

The little girl conducted them into a back room, in which were a few scanty pieces of furniture, and a bed, upon which was propped up with pillows a sick woman, engaged in sewing. Her face was pale and thin, and her eyes, bright and glistening, were sunk far into her head. The work dropped from her hand as her unexpected visitors entered, and then she looked up earnestly into the face of the elder of the two.

"You do not seem able to work, ma'am," said Jane's mother, advancing to the bedside, and taking the small, thin hand that was offered her.

"I am not very able, ma'am," she replied in a feeble tone. "But I have to do something."

"Is there no one to provide any thing for you, in your feeble state?" asked her visitor.

"No one, ma'am," was the simple, and, to Jane's mother, affecting response.

"And how many hours through the day do you have to sit up in bed and sew?"

"All day, when I can, ma'am. And sometimes a good many hours at night.

But I wouldn't care so much for that, if I was able to go about the room a little, and attend more to my child, who is, indeed, sadly neglected." And the tears came into the mother's eyes, as she cast a look of tenderness upon her little girl.

Jane saw that look, and noted the sad expression of the poor woman's voice, and both touched her heart.

"Cannot we do something for them?" she whispered.

"We must try," was the low response.

"I heard of your being ill this morning," Jane's mother said, "and have come over to see if I can do any thing for you. You must be relieved from your constant labour, for it is too much for your feeble frame. As soon as I return home, I will send you over as much food as you and your little girl will require for several days, and my daughter here will be willing, I think, to come in to see you now and then, and give you such little assistance as you may require. Will you not, Jane?"

"Oh yes, mother. I will come most cheerfully." And the tone of her voice, and expression of her face showed that she was in earnest.

The poor woman could not find words to speak out her true feelings, but she looked her gratitude.

After Jane and her mother had left this miserable tenement, the former said—

"O mother, it makes my heart ache to think of that poor woman and her child! How can she possibly get bread to eat, by the work of her own hands, and she almost dying?"

The sympathy thus expressed pleased her mother very much, and she encouraged the good impression. After she had returned home, she prepared a number of articles of food, such as she thought were required, and also a few delicacies that she knew would be grateful to the sick woman. These she despatched by a servant. About half an hour after, Jane, with a small bundle in her hand, went out alone, and turned her steps toward the cheerless hovel she had but a short time before visited. In this bundle was a change of clothing for the invalid, which Jane assisted her to put on. And then she made up her bed for her, and beat up the pillows, and fixed her as comfortably as possible.

Then she took the little girl, and washed her, and combed her hair, and put on a clean frock that her mother told her she would find in a closet. After this she arranged every thing in the room in order, and swept up the floor. And still further, went to work and got a nice cup of tea for the sick woman.

It would have done the heart of any one good to have seen how full of delight and gratitude was the countenance of the sick woman. Jane had never felt so happy in her life.

When she came home, her mother remarked her light step and cheerful air.

"You have at last learned how to be happy, Jane," said she. "The secret lies in our endeavouring to be useful to others. All our unhappiness springs from some indulgence of selfishness, and all our true feelings of happiness from that benevolence which prompts us to regard others."

Jane saw and felt the force of her mother's remark, and never forgot it. The sick woman, in whom she had become interested, afforded ample scope for the exercise of her newly awakened feelings of benevolence, and thus they gained strength and grew into principles of action. May every one who reads this little story find the true secret of happiness!

# THE OLD MAN AT THE COTTAGE-DOOR.

COME, faint old man! and sit awhile
  Beside our cottage-door;
A cup of water from the spring,
  A loaf to bless the poor,
We give with cheerful hearts, for God
  Hath given us of his store.

Too feeble thou for daily toil,
  Too weak to earn thy bread—
For the weight of many, many years
  Lies heavy on thy head—
A wanderer, Want thy weary feet
  Hath to our cottage led.

Come, rest awhile. 'Twill not be long,
  Ere thy faint head shall know

THE OLD MAN AT THE COTTAGE DOOR.

(10) Page 126.

A deeper, calmer, better rest,
  Than cometh here below;
When God, who loveth every one,
  Shall call thee hence to go.

Heaven bless thee in thy wanderings!
  Wherever they may be,
And make the ears of every one
  Attentive to thy plea:
A double blessing will be theirs,
  Who kindly turn to thee.

# THE LITTLE BOY WHO HAD LEARNED HIS LESSON.

"YOU seem quite happy, my son," said a father to his little boy, who came in from the garden singing merrily. "What have you been doing?"

"I've been playing in the garden ever since I got my lesson, papa."

"Then you've got your lesson for to-morrow? Do you know it well?"

"Oh yes, I know every word."

"Do you always know your lessons?" asked the father.

"Not always; but I'm going to try and get them well after this."

"Ah, indeed! I'm glad to hear that,

Charlie. How long since you made this good resolution?"

"Ever since yesterday. I didn't see any use in studying, until mother told us that if we didn't learn all we could, we would not be able, when we grew up to be men, to do as much good to others as we might have done; for we all had to do good to others, and that, if we didn't do it, we would never go to heaven and become angels."

Charlie's father felt very glad to hear his little boy say this. He lifted him up and kissed him, and said—

"If you always try and get your lessons well, that you may learn how to do good to others, you will surely become an angel when you go out of this world. The angels are employed only in doing good, and all who love to do good on this earth become angels in heaven when they die."

## LITTLE CHILDREN.

"WHEN the Lord of life and glory
Came, from sin to set us free,
He smiled on the weak ones, saying—
Little children, come to me.

In his arms He kindly took them,
And upon each infant head
Laid His holy hands, and blessings—
Heavenly blessings—on them shed.

"Suffer ye the little children,"
He to his disciples said,
"Thus to come: of such my Kingdom
In the heavens and earth is made.

"All who follow me must humbly,
Even as a little child,
Bear my light and easy burden,
Meekly own my precepts mild."

Little children, still the Saviour
Wooes you to his kind embrace;
Still he says, "Come, little children,
Come and see my smiling face.

"Banish every bad affection,
Evil thoughts keep far away,
And my angels, sent from heaven,
Near you all the while shall stay.

"They behold my face and glory,
They the love I bear you know,
And, upon their work of mercy,
Fill'd with heavenly gladness, go."

Then be joyful, little children—
Even in sorrow, joyful be—
Angel-guards are all around you,
Moved by heavenly sympathy.

E'en though, urged by wicked spirits,
  Cruel men your bodies tear,
Yield not up to thoughts of evil:
  Seek, then, seek the Lord in prayer.

Very near he'll then be to you,
  And he'll wipe your tears away:
Little children, when forsaken,
  And in trouble, learn to pray.

## THE LITTLE WORD "NO."

"THERE is a word, my son, a very little word, in the English language, the right use of which it is all-important that you should learn," said Mr. Howland to his son Thomas, who was about leaving the paternal roof for a residence in a neighbouring city, never again, perchance, to make one of the little circle that had so long gathered in the family homestead.

"And what word is that, father?" asked Thomas.

"It is the little word *No*, my son."

"And why does so much importance attach to that word, father?"

"Perhaps I can make you understand the

L 2

reason much better if I relate an incident that occurred when I was a boy. I remember it as distinctly as if it had taken place but yesterday, although thirty years have since passed. There was a neighbour of my father's who was very fond of gunning and fishing. On several occasions, I had accompanied him, and had enjoyed myself very much. One day, my father said to me—

"'William, I do not wish you to go into the woods or on the water again with Mr. Jones.'

"'Why not, father?' I asked, for I had become so fond of going with him, that to be denied the pleasure was a real privation.

"'I have good reasons for not wishing you to go, William,' my father replied, 'but do not want to give them now. I hope it is all-sufficient for you, that your father desires you not to accompany Mr. Jones again.'

"I could not understand why my father laid upon me this prohibition; and, as I desired very much to go, I did not feel satisfied in my obedience. On the next day, as I was walking along the road, I met Mr. Jones, with his fishing-rod on his shoulder and his basket in his hand.

"'Ah, William! you are the very one that I wished to see,' said Mr. Jones smiling. 'I am going out this morning, and want company. We shall have a beautiful day.'

"'But my father told me yesterday,' I replied, 'that he did not wish me to go out with you.'

"'And why not, pray?' asked Mr. Jones.

"'I am sure that I do not know,' said I; 'but, indeed, I should like to go very much.'

"'Oh, never mind; come along,' said he. 'Your father will never know it.'

"'Yes, but I am afraid that he will,' I replied, thinking more of my father's displeasure than of the evil of disobedience.

"'There is no danger at all of that.

We will be home again long before dinner-time.'

"I hesitated, and he urged; and finally, I moved the way that he was going, and had proceeded a few hundred yards, when I stopped and said—

"'I don't like to go, Mr. Jones.'

"'Nonsense, William! There is no harm in fishing, I am sure. I have often been out with your father, myself.'

"Much as I felt inclined to go, still I hesitated; for I could not fully make up my mind to disobey my father. At length he said—

"'I can't wait here for you, William. Come along, or go back. Say yes, or no.'

"This was the decisive moment. I was to make up my mind, and fix my determination in one way or the other. I was to say *yes* or NO.

"'Come, I can't stay here all day,' Mr. Jones remarked rather harshly, seeing that I hesitated. At the same moment, the image of my father rose distinctly before my mind, and I saw his eye fixed steadily and reprovingly upon me. With one desperate resolution, I uttered the word—

"'No!' and then turning, ran away as fast as my feet would carry me. I cannot tell you how much relieved I felt when I was far beyond the reach of temptation.

"On the next morning, when I came down to breakfast, I was startled and surprised to learn that Mr. Jones had been drowned on the day before. Instead of returning in a few hours, as he had stated to me that he would, he remained out all day. A sudden storm arose; his boat was capsized, and he drowned. I shuddered when I heard this sad and fatal accident related. That little word NO had, in all probability, saved my life.

"'I will now tell you, William,' my father said, turning to me, 'why I did not wish you to go with Mr. Jones. Of late he had taken to drinking; and I had learned, within a few days, that whenever he went out on a fishing or gunning excursion, he took his bottle of spirits with him, and usually returned a good deal intoxicated. I could not trust you with such a man. I did not think it necessary to state this to you, for I was sure that I had only to express my wish that you would not accompany him, to insure your implicit obedience.'

"I felt keenly rebuked at this; and resolved never again to permit even the thought of disobedience to find a place in my mind. From that time I have felt the value of the word NO, and have generally, ever since, been able to use it on all right occasions. It has saved me from many troubles. Often and often in life have I been urged to do things that my judgment told me were wrong: on such occasions, I always remember my first temptation, and resolutely said—

"'No!'

"And now, my son," continued Mr. Howland, "do you understand the importance of the word *No?*"

"I think I do, father," replied Thomas. "But is there not danger of my using it too often, and thus becoming selfish in all my feelings, and, consequently, unwilling to render benefits to others?"

"Certainly there is, Thomas. The right use of this word is to resist evil. To refuse to do a good action is wrong."

"If any one asks me, then, to do him a favour, or kindness, I should not, on any account, say no."

"That will depend, Thomas, in what manner you are to render him a kindness. If you can do so without really injuring yourself or others, then it is a duty which you owe to all men, to be kind, and render favours."

"But the difficulty, I feel, will be for me to discriminate. When I am urged to do something by one whom I esteem, my regard for him, or my desire to render him an obligation, will be so strong as to obscure my judgment."

"A consciousness of this weakness in

your character, Thomas, should put you upon your guard."

"That is very true, father. But I cannot help fearing for myself. Still, I shall never forget what you have said, and will try my best to act from a conviction of right."

"Do so, my son. And ever remember, that a wrong action is *always* followed by pain of mind, and very frequently by evil consequences. If you would avoid these, ever act from a consciousness that you are doing right, without regard to others. If another asks you, from a selfish desire to benefit or gratify himself, to do what your judgment tells you is wrong, surely you should have no hesitation in refusing."

The precept of his father, enforced when they were about parting, and at a time when his affection for that father was active and intense, lingered in the mind of Thomas Howland. He saw and felt its force, and resolved to act in obedience to it, if ever tempted to do wrong.

On leaving the paternal roof, he went to a neighbouring town, and entered the store of a merchant, where were several young men nearly of his own age, that is, between eighteen and twenty. With one of these, named Boyd, he soon formed an intimate acquaintance. But, unfortunately, the moral character of this young man was far from being pure, or his principles from resting upon the firm basis of truth and honor.

His growing influence over Thomas Howland was apparent in inducing him to stay away from church on the Sabbath-day, and pass the time that had heretofore been spent in a place of worship, in roaming about the wharves of the city, or in excursions into the country. This influence was slightly resisted; but Thomas felt ashamed or reluctant to use the word "*No*" on what seemed to all the young men around him a a matter of so little importance. Still, his own heart condemned him, for he felt that it would pain his father and mother exceedingly if they knew that he neglected to attend church at least once on the Sabbath-day—and he was, besides, self convicted of wrong in what seemed to him a violation of the precept, *Remember the Sabbath-day*, &c., as he had been taught to regard that precept. But once having given way, he felt almost powerless to resist the influence that now bore upon him.

The next violation of what seemed to him a right course for a young man to pursue, was in suffering himself to be persuaded to visit frequently the theatre; although his father had expressly desired that he would avoid a place where lurked for the young and inexperienced so many dangers. He was next easily persuaded to visit a favourite eating-house, in which many hours were spent during the evenings of each week, with Boyd and others, in eating, drinking, and smoking. Sometimes dominos and back-gammon were introduced, and at length were played for a slight stake. To participate in this Thomas refused, on the plea that he did not know enough of the games to risk any thing. He had not the moral courage to declare that he considered it wrong to gamble.

All these departures from what he had been taught by his father to consider a right course, were attended by much uneasiness and pain of mind. But he had yielded to the tempter, and he could not now find the power within him to resist his influence successfully.

It happened, about six months after his introduction to such an entirely new course of life, that he was invited one evening by his companion Boyd, to call on a friend with him. He had, on that day, received from his father forty dollars, with which to buy himself a new suit of clothes, and a few other necessary articles. He went, of course, and was introduced to a very affable, gentlemanly young man, in his room, at one of the hotels. In a few minutes, wine and cigars were ordered, and the three spent an hour or so, in drinking, smoking, and chitchat of no very elevating or refined character.

"Come, let us have a game of cards," the friend at last remarked, during a pause in the conversation; at the same time going to his trunk and producing a pack of cards.

"No objection," responded Boyd.

"You'll take a hand, of course?" the new friend said, looking at Thomas Howland.

But Thomas said that he knew nothing of cards.

"Oh, that's no matter! You can learn in two minutes," responded the friend of Boyd.

Young Howland felt reluctant, but he could not resist the influence that was around him, and so he consented to finger the cards with the rest. As they gathered around the table, a half-dollar was laid down by each of the young men, who looked toward Thomas as they did so.

"I cannot play for money," said he, colouring; for he felt really ashamed to acknowledge his scruples.

"And why not?" asked the friend of Boyd, looking him steadily in the face.

"Because I think it wrong," stammered out Howland, colouring still more deeply.

"Nonsense! Isn't your money your own? And pray what harm is there in your doing with your own as you please?" urged the tempter.

"But I do not know enough of the game to risk my money."

"You don't think we would take advantage of your ignorance?" said Boyd. "The stake is only to give interest to the game. I would not give a copper for a game of cards without a stake. Come, put down your half-dollar, and we'll promise to pay you back all you lose, if you wish it, until you acquire some skill."

But Thomas felt reluctant and hesitated. Nevertheless, he was debating the matter in his mind seriously, and every moment that reluctance was growing weaker.

"Will you play?" asked Boyd in a decided tone, breaking in upon this debate.

"I had rather not," Thomas replied, attempting to smile, so as to conciliate his false friends.

"You are afraid of your money," said Boyd in a half-sneering tone.

"It is not that, Boyd."

"Then what is it, pray?"

"I am afraid that it is not right."

This was answered by a loud laugh from his two friends, which touched Thomas a good deal, and made him feel more ashamed of the scruples that held him back from entering into the temptation.

"Come, down with your stake, Howland!" said Boyd, after he had finished his laugh.

The hand of Thomas was in his pocket, and his fingers had grasped the silver coin, yet still he hesitated.

"Will you play or not?" the friend of Boyd now said, with something of impatience in his tone. "Say yes or no?"

For a moment the mind of Thomas became confused—then the perception came upon him, as clear as a sunbeam, that it was wrong to gamble. He remembered, too, vividly his father's parting injunction.

"*No!*" said he, firmly and decidedly.

Both of his companions looked disappointed and angry.

"What did you bring him here, for?" he heard Boyd's companion say to him in an under tone, while a frown darkened upon his brow.

The reply did not reach his ear, but he felt that his company was no longer pleasant; and rising, he bade them a formal good-evening, and hurriedly retired. That little word *no* had saved him. The scheme was, to win from him his forty dollars, and then involve him in "debts of honour," as they are falsely called, which would compel him to draw upon his father for more money, or abstract it from his employer, a system which had been pursued by Boyd, and which was discovered only a week subsequent, when the young man was discharged in disgrace. It then came out, that he had been for months in secret association with a gambler, and that the two shared together their spoils and speculations.

This incident aroused Thomas Howland to a distinct consciousness of the danger that lurked in his path, as a young man in a large city. He felt, as he had not felt while simply listening to his father's precept, the value of the word *No;* and resolved that, hereafter, he would utter that little word, and that, too, decidedly, whenever urged to do what his judgment did not approve.

"I will be free!" said he, pacing his chamber backward and forward. "I will be free, hereafter! No one shall persuade me or drive me to do what I feel to be wrong."

That resolution was his safeguard ever after. When tempted, and he was tempted frequently, his "*No*" decided the matter at once. There was a power in it that was all-sufficient in resisting evil.

# A VALENTINE.

MY carrier-dove, dear Alice!
I send this day to you,
With silken cords and words of love,
And heart as warm as true.

I would not trust the butterfly,
These tokens, love, to bring,
Lest some sweet flow'r should tempt the wight
To fold his gauzy wing.

Ah! never trust the butterfly,
Though on the summer air
He moves with such a gentle grace—
He's fickle as he's fair.

Some pure young blossom now he wooes
With many a tender word,
And now the heartless eloquence
Another flower has heard.

---

But in the constant dove confide,
So gentle, loving, true;
Not 'mid the gay, bright garden's bloom
Comes this sweet friend to you.

Not in the bower, where clustering hang
The treasures of the vine,
But where the golden beams of day
Mid quiet groves decline.

Dear Alice! let the emblems
That now to you I send,
Their lessons on your thoughts impress,
And with your feelings blend.

Be true and constant, like the dove,
And let love's fetters bind
Your heart in generous sympathy
To all of human kind.

THE END.

STEREOTYPED BY L. JOHNSON & CO.
PHILADELPHIA.

www.ingramcontent.com/pod-product-compliance
Lightning Source LLC
LaVergne TN
LVHW021408110826
845150LV00007B/1829